Each Chartered Street

Sebastian Agudelo

saturnalia books

Distributed by University Press of New England
Hanover and London

Saturnalia Books
105 Woodside Rd.
Ardmore, PA 19003
info@saturnaliabooks.com

ISBN: 978-0-9833686-9-4
Library of Congress Control Number: 2013947565

Book Design by EJ Herczyk
Printing by The Prolific Group, Canada

Cover Art: Image by Lia Kantrowitz

Author Photo: K. Mach

Distributed by:
University Press of New England
1 Court Street
Lebanon, NH 03766
800-421-1561

Thanks to the editors of the following journals for first publishing some of this poems, sometimes in different versions: *American Poetry Review*: "The Consolations of Philosphy," "Salvage," "Block Party"; *At Length*: "Commute"; *Antioch Review*: "Testimony"; *Beloit Poetry Journal*: "Summary"; *Fogged Clarity*: "The Wisdom of the Ancients"; *The Manchester Review*: "Knowledge," "Black Vesper's Pageants," "Memorial."

For Katharina and Madeleine

Table of Contents

"però che 'l loco u' fui a viver posto,
di giorno in giorno più di ben si spopla,
e a trista ruina par disposto."
—Purgatorio

Those born and blessed by fortune
cannot know what's brooked
by those who run the outermost roads of elsewhere.

—The Seafarer
(James Langer, trans.)

I

Knowledge

is one thing to the middle-age guy
crossing checkboxes in the food court
printing BA for highest degree earned
in a job application for Salad Works;

another for the kids spread out
two tables down, going back and forth
from cell phone to school work.
One, a high-tech, lovelorn schmuck

waiting for a love note, smudged
the screen ten times at least, keyed in
passcode, scrolled down, up, down
to come up empty, I guess, the way

he quickly pressed the sleep button,
put the thing down. Another one
flipped her Blackberry three times,
just to let it rest face down and

mop her textbook with highlighters.
She'll wash whole pages in so much
see-through fluorescence, let soul slip
in its dark night, it would startle, freeze

like stag in headlights. I see those guys,
big guys, who turn to a reflective strip,
bob in the tunnel, fade to air horn's blast.
So I guess to me the soul is flicker

of indeterminate work, with track rats,
danger, dirt. These kids, like clerks
with pricing guns on clearance,
chisel tip and color-code whatever

comes their way: pink for the gunners
on the dock-board track at Passchendale,
purple for genocides, green all over
Dustbowl, yellow for Black Tuesdays.

They'll trim the bitumen of ziggurat,
patch the cracks of Wailing Wall with
Lego-like chromatics, hedge famines
tidying the take over of tuff and weed,

where knowing begins, as cockspur overgrows
Empire's crop and anything will do, fryer, mop…
Ask the guy who's moved down another
franchise and is thinking mortgage, food.

He would color-code, if at all, like a snake
licking the odor from the air just to get
a quick quiver in the threshold of infrared
which means disquiet, heat, blow, meat.

History

(After Juan Gelman)

Flip through it, BC to AD,
from chromosomal Adam
to your company man,
the countdown to messiahs,
the forward of Juggernauts.
There are letters chiseled
on stone: *the city's fate*
cannot be determined, says one,
its book-keeper is a merchant.
Afterwards: the name exists
but the place has been destroyed.
Think, Thermopylae to Fallujah,
histrionics, purple passages,
dogmas to make martyrs bleed,
courts, tribunals, auto-da-fes.
From first time tragedy to
the farcical reruns, past
gridirons, rubber hoses, garrotes,
through so much smoke rising
there's one stay: thickened,
crooked, near cairn or loom,
threading, delving, the hands,
myth says—for good reason—
buried, still grow nails.

The Consolations of Philosophy

That the cicada is the mercy of the muse,
  our birth but sleep and forgetting,
that the body dizzies in a realm of the variable.

  Plato in the elevator, as good a place
as any I guess, to ponder soul's madness,
  the den of ignorance, the wash

and opacity that's the day to day, the lives
  on trees and shrubs. As good a place,
and this emo, dweebish, Gothy girl has

  her nose buried in it, a cinderblock
worth of dialogues, truth, goodness, the just
  lumbered by crime and outrage.

Not that distant, the world doors open to
  the republic, or another iteration of it.
Its sail is still too large, its body overfed.

  Grasping oligarchs prattle on split
plasma screens bracketed everywhere, a mock
  dialectic, muted and close-captioned

for any to see Glaucon's eulogists of injustice
  transmigrated and hamming it up
on FOX or CNN, like sportscasters of blood-

  sport on the round-up of the game,
tallying spoil and foul and screw-up for travelers
  waiting in gates or shoving paperwork.

Here's how the republic's servants make do:
  some are too old to serve, border guards
of a kind, pitched behind lecterns, nodding

    sharp, jerky nods, passport to face
  and back, behind monitors also, by metal
    detectors that spike to small change

key chains, belt buckles, money clips.
    They bounce folks out to get it right,
hand them a gray tub to empty pockets in,

    shepherd them through once more
  while the conveyor belt feeds its tunnel
    the pile-up of bags, coats, shoes.

Enough about them, our keepers. What
    they keep is gridlocked, backing-up
past the cordoned off area: teenagers in sweats

    lugging pillows, kids glued to the 3-D
  drive-by shootings their PlayStations replicate,
    bags bulging, inflatables, stuffed toys,

panda, puppy, platypus, all in an amnion of
    ear buds, synthesized chime, ping, jingle.
Some are saying their goodbyes; most just

    fidget, text, twiddle, shift their weight,
  can't wait to get through, edging totes
    and duffels with their feet another inch.

In Plato, they'd be lovers of sight and sound,
   their ears to every chorus at the Dionysiac,
unfit to rule or figure what is true.

   The cave is branded and trademarked
for the skillful physicians of the State
   to brew their strong dose of falsehood.

They're a mob themselves, wanting to steer,
   clueless of the art, too baffled to look up
and see the stars. She's managed to keep

   going at it all along, cramming for a test,
thirsting for knowledge, *Rainbow Girl,* she's
   written with metallic ink all over her backpack.

On the screen, some corn-fed Beltway bully
   panders for the gifts from Merk or Wyeth
uniquely American solutions, caption reads.

   We're edging nearer. *Leave the subtleties
to others, Callicles says. Envy those who have.*
   A view the guy three places ahead

seems to embrace judging from the spate
   of electronics he's unhooking, peeling away
and unloading from his corporate carry-on.

   And who landed the contract for those gray
tubs anyway? Callicles alleged point being,
   thought's logical outcomes were the *abjurals*

from *the city and its meeting places, a life*
of refutals, the undoing of mankind,
the sapping away of our practical wherewithals.

A point best made by *Rainbow Girl,* who
puts Complete Dialogues and backpack in
a tub. So absorbed in poring over virtue,

or whatnot, her shoes are on still, and turns
out the long skirt was concealing a pair
of purple knee-high tennis boots, fifty

or sixty eyelets per shoe. You could hear
the disaffected chitchat zero in on scapegoat,
You've gotta be fucking kidding me,

the cue delivered stadium-voice somewhere
from behind, and the TSA men more
acquainted with the leaven of the mob,

go preemptory on the guy. Hum simmers
nonetheless. *Leirios,* lily-like translation
has it, what summer's canopy will echo

from the cicada's thoracic contraction
and release. That in some manic enrapture,
some euphoric seventh heaven, seized

on the cloud nine of drive and momentum,
men died without knowing and woke
to be molting sentinels, lulling men to stupor.

The mercies of the muse. That state have gadfly.
   The banner at the top is scrolling indices,
futures dropped. On the bottom, the debate

   goes on, *I object...I object...I object.*
The caption as if stuck, senator in a tantrum.
   That the true answer to the question

is relative to circumstance. That our argument
   has turned like a person making fun of us.
That to the god of healing we owe cock.

The Wisdom of the Ancients

What country is this? Oedipus stumbles
at the threshold, on his way out, his last job.

You feel for him even if you're neither old
nor blind, just waking to the headlines.

What country? The neo-Nazi baby showers,
BBQ's with aging KKK's, munitions

stockpiled in some California basement
where, about right now, they're lifting

prints, have handcuffed the ten year old
who shot his white supremacist dad.

What country. And that's just one instance
gone awry in the freak show of grievance

and discontent, all very justified, if misguided.
In the morning paper, the mighty purse

their lips, so serious, so worried, so…
To stay the part they must re-run

Doomsday tsunamis in their heads,
imagine tax havens sinking like Atlantis.

The crowd throngs around Oedipus
who tramples the manicured grounds

of shrine, steps in the wrong place,
considering the blesséd ones underground

are chartered to avenge the very crimes
he's guilty of. The crowd is wary, touchy,

territorial, the sort of throng that hovers
near the wounded, vacillates—in full choric sway—

between taking the thing out of its misery
or picking it up, offer alms or arms.

Nothing as bad as what I've seen of late,
the proud man's contumely in full display,

on Broad and Walnut, where walking past
one of those guys who've broad-tipped

abridged bio on cardboard, begging for change
(Iraq Vet, HIV positive, hungry) the boss

of the window washing crew turned around
and began to pelt the beggar, hard,

a pocket-full of loose change, penny by penny.
What country. Everyone a paycheck away

from the curb; everyone, the best still,
quick for illegal turns. Them and them alone.

Who was the man? Where has he gone?...
A bum, a beggar, not of this place, the chorus

asks in unison. *Were you born like this?*
Born for this? Then, I'll be damned if you

bring down this curse of yours on us. They'll relax,
begin to *oh* and *ah* along with him,

welcome him eventually, proud of country,
rich and strong. *Whose city is this?* asks Oedipus,

learning to be easy with whatever happens,
resigned with every crime committed.

He is a man come to die, trying to wipe clean
a rap sheet that has it all, parricide,

regicide, incest, worse, the sheer insolent
pride that got him here in the first place

and though there's greatness in him,
we're supposed to glean an exemplar

of what the human is, not just the smarts
to down the idols a city is beholden to,

but the way your finest moment will do
that volte-face and turn out a fuck up really

with a mighty comeuppance as a prize.
Here he is, worn out, impaired, needing pity.

My students don't or won't care or get it.
They're getting the news from *gradesaver.com*

There are some hints of sadness in the poem
one of them cuts and pastes, continues

The narcissus is the symbolic flower of death—
the plagiarist. Them and them alone,

quick enough for the illegal moves,
invulnerable, blessed, in a rich country.

Oedipus will wend his way into the thicket
that keeps the daughters of the dark,

threshold to a city, its very border.
Today is his last day. He's on the know,

his turn to tease with riddles: *Whose country,*
whose city is this? No answer. Them alone.

Commute

i.

On the platform, blood and wing bones
like the leavings from some Obeah jinx.
A kid's tutu on the tracks.

In the air, urine and cold cream,
overheard talk the train drowns
as it lumbers, whines and bangs open.

On, to where Virginia Woolf confined
her progeny, the *novelists in the future,*
omnibuses and underground railways.

Via Crucis or way of virtue, she won't say
nor venture what flash fictions or elliptic
avants will birth, hallows on instead

these the depths they will explore,
those the phantoms they'll pursue.
Superimposed, shallow with detail

punctuated by the intermittent fade out
as the tunnel lights strobe in, bleached
by station lights, poor contorted devils sit,

the penitent stand and hold on—
souls ferried, back and forth,
to the mild prosaic hells of shifts.

The Russian hairdresser preps through
a box full of flashcards for the GED.
The Chicana *au pair* beside her nods,

nods, nods, then straightens up to cross
herself. The kid bound for Temple
or CCP, draped in insurrection-chic keffiyeh

is doing the Analects. It's early morning
when secretaries page through catalogs
and touch up their make-up or dog-ear magazines.

I stick to the syllabus, Montaigne today
(the worst of these wars is that the cards are so mixed-up)
and haul a bagful of anthologies from place to place

like lackey to a sales-rep from Norton or Wiley,
but worse, in the paycheck-to-paycheck
gestarbeiter to higher-ed, contracted in four

stops of the line. What pays the bills?
…This world of ours is the looking glass…
…We're fashioned of oddments put together…

I drift to tinny hip-hop. It sizzles
from the speaker of a clamshell phone
a woman by the door wedged

to the hem of her *purdah*. She's beneath
the sign: no food, no smoking, no radios,
broadcasting in the musical counterpart

to the sputtery fizz of police radio
only a back up track to her larger message.
…Time and custom condition us to anything strange…

ii.

Later, I'll be northbound with Robert Browning
or Robert Frost, the crowd thinned out
to the unemployable and unemployed.
They file through paperwork, applications,
printouts with rooms for rent.
They rifle through insurance forms,
analysis results, documents for their PO.
Later still, I'm southbound when Catholic school
kids hop in and peel off ties and v-necks.
No black bough for petals to bloom
like *sumi-e* in the squalor of the Metro.
Scrap also the photo-realist, funhouse
mirrors in Este's urban jigsaws,
the convex of handrail, slight distortions
on a dented door, the sanitized glare
of the hyper-real, that O.R.-look.
The window-shaped guise of myself
is sebumgray and curd, a spat-on tag
slashes where I superimpose on Diablo,
on the phone, beneath ads
for deodorants and loan sharks.
He's tattooed his *nom de plume* on one
side of his neck and notched his street cred
with tears shaped like dollar signs.
From behind his ear, across his nape
and to the other ear, he's inked Requiescats
to all his fallen—so far. He's going
to the morgue, has the *Daily News* open
to the crime report. I'm not making him up,
just tallying the odds that last night's pop-off
on Marion street might be the tattoo parlor's
next job, just charting how wide or narrow
a semantic radius tells near from close.

iii.

(We know the uncle—a kid in his twenties really—
who moved in to help, one of those houses where
the nucleus in the nuclear of the "family"
has this blobby, inchoate, pliancy, all absorption,

all resilience, all about making the rent,
however crowded, however Children of Sanchez
slummy the whole arrangement ends up.
He worked at the depot for awhile.

I'd see him mornings, waiting for the bus
in his groomed unbuttoned back-brace cool.
Then he vanished, served time, came back—
his belongings in a garbage bag, bloated

from drink and with a new set of contacts
in his phone, to set up shop, run a live corner
where Marion dead-ends on Queen Lane.
Or so it seemed, his loitering hours on end,

that aimless orbiting, that antsy twinge
of the lookout, then a crew regathering,
the boss with his black dog, two other guys
checking in before they'd walk down

on Marion, to the stash house which
after one a.m. was awash in beacon light,
one Rashid Olmstead shot three times.
Not that Diablo need be know associate, but...)

iv.

They're neighbors, after all, the folk I ride with,
though I covet nothing from them.
Not distracted from distraction by distraction,
swamped, ill-used, with strollers and walkers to fight.
They're hoping for salvation and the big bucks.
They read the Watchtower or scrape the latex
of scratch-and-wins, Royal Riches, Instant Millions.
One folds the winning tickets and tosses the rest.
They're mainly uniformed, with franchise polos,
the name-tag in style, upside down
and pinned to the cap worn backward,
for Willie, at least. Others wear piped trousers
and untucked, white-shirts with epaulettes,
stitched with an outfit's logo, *Securitas,*
Sovereign, Scotland Yard. So many, you figure
every lobby under siege. Some have commando
sweaters, badges, duty belts, as ornamental
as their jobs. *Novelists in the future,* pay heed,
their shift could be the mouth-to-mouth
that brings the *Nouveau Roman* back to life,
milk the existential in a chapter that transcribes
the gabble of the walkie-talkie on its charger.
Then a chapter to each screen as it multiplies
the doldrums of office jobs, the stasis of hall,
the inertia in storage rooms, the poetry in back-lots.

v.

Montaigne says *the most equitable polities*
allow least inequality between servants and
masters, but Amy will check for split ends
on a hime cut that has its own budget
on shampoo and conditioner alone.

Montaigne says the cannibal on tour
took note that *amongst us, men fully bloated*
with all kinds of comfort have their halves
begging at their doors. Ryan licks his thumb
and rubs the skid mark off his trainers.

Montaigne asks *how many trades*
and vocations gain acceptance
whose very essence is vicious? Anyone?
I'm pacing book in hand
shut out by blank stares.

Montaigne says. I go through zingers,
underlines, back-track to anecdote.
Equitable polities? They want to know
what's on the test, to go on to their lives,
pay tuition, wait tables, work for tips.

vi.

On the platform, as usual, the wet floor
sandwich boards every few feet,
their functionalist, pared down pictogram

stuck in the eternity of mid-skid.
Their everyman, our psycho pomp to mishap
steers us from the spill and signals

where straw rusticles drip from rebar
like pins to map infrastructure
breaking down, the cracks in our foundation.

I'm homebound with my own Q&A,
my own multiple-choice quiz
not just the usual *what'a fuck?* after a bad class.

Did they read? Do they care? What do I care?
Nor the who's first in an inbox that gathers
neglect like a bad conscience, but the more

inarticulate thread that catches in small ache,
a shoulder say, but seems to unravel
like cause and effect gone berserk

through every incidental that brought
ache in the first place, bad sleep, no insurance,
overdue bills, the twenty pounds worth

of Western canon from Homer to Heaney
I cram in my bag each day.
Jeune Homme Triste Dans Un Train?

Not so *jeune* and not so *triste*, more the burnout
that Archbishop blesses as resilience and Deans
look down upon; they ought to know.

The CNA in front of me wears my own aura
and might say *I'll cure you, measure out your dose
but want you gone, my overtime, my cross to bear.*

vii.

Novelists,

From overseen Tweets and Facebook
postings you'll gather the seeds to the next
epistolary saga of a girl lost in the big city.

If video game characters were real people,
I would want to fuck so many of them.

God if the douche bag grabs my ass
in front of a customer one more goddamned time ....

La Cucaracha on xylophone. Chewbacca roars.
Celine, Whitney or Mariah belt melismas.

In the afterlings of confession that follow ringtone
you'll sound a whole *Bildungsroman.*

No, no little boy I'm not playing with you Fabree,
leave that faggot alone, unfriend him, he is a pervert.

Or reconstitute a picaresque from the husks
of minister bargaining with some politico
on the other side. *Darnell is a good kid.*
He is calling in a favor; he's kept score, the canvassing,
how he brought the congregation down to vote,
shifts to the kid. *The kid's a good kid, a real good kid,*
maybe you find him a spot. In another place,

this is father phoning in admissions, shopping
for a better school but here we dead end so fast
at hearings, arraignment, court. It's your next
Lazarillo, a fresh Don Pablo with up-to-date thieves' cant.

viii.

Conversely, one might opt against
the odd details in pure surface,
keep the anti-novel at bay,
ditch picaresque, epistolary, coming of age
and go for the *real unexaggerated lion,*
the rounded backs, the stupid weather-beaten faces,
the work-worn hands, Eliot's vulgar citizen,
her common laborer with his *vulgar eating.*

The bill of fare these starving souls unwrap
would be more than enough.
It wafts from foil and Styrofoam,
the type 2 diabetes, the quintuple bypass
they pick up on-the-go on Broad and Erie
where we transfer to any of the seven routes
that converge here and a moraine of makeshift
stands has washed across the sidewalk.
Rocks, twine, tarp, crates, stretched metal
to display the wares, the do-or-die
carnivalesque of sub- or unemployment:
burned DVDs, new releases sure, but also
Barely Legal, Almost Jailbait, Sodomize This.
Contraband, knock-offs, umbrellas, hats.

Why not hope for realism's solace?
Why not wish, despite the squalor
and cruelty there, Brueghel's folksy touch
diffuse its insights on the scene,
what he knew about suffering, sure,

but also how lands of plenty cloy,
how his bookkeeper dozes,
law and order go down for the count,
the salve of proverb, the dignity of fools.
Despite the squeal and blare and tweedle,
despite their demented spot-the-difference
roughneck broil, their tear-rouges, outcriers,
the *ad libitum* charivari of kettle, pan and tray.

ix.

Instead, sedans throb by like heart attacks,
gangs of kids on ATV's rip by this Vegas bone yard-
worth of broken bulb-signs hanging by their last,
the ruined mortal and pestle Rx
of an unincorporated pharmacy shut down.

Here apothecary, packing, ministers his cure
in vial and dime bag, slings beside the church
where the bilingual banner stretched across
the façade promises to fend *envy, evil eye.*
Fruits of the Spirit sells produce in a bag.

Instead, jaundice colors in the emaciated
we know from Evans and Lang
and much of where I came from bleeds
to where I am, no fire eaters, street clowns
kids sniffing glue. Not yet. Still, it's Ubar,

Vilcambaba, Palenque in the make with the looks
of squatter city, that sort of stop-gap
rigging, ragged scaffolding, crumpled tin
that the dereliction of the haves seems to squeeze
out everywhere, Rio, Mumbai, Cape Town.

Here, the comma of a curved arrow sign
points, not nowhere, but to the ill-
starred, late-capitalist nowhere of the cement
roughcast that condemns the window of a former bank.
And samaras whirl their way to gutter.

One thrived. Its sapling corkscrews
and leans out to touch the powerlines.
Palenque in the make, ready for its Maudslay
come lift prints. The bookstore *Ships to Prison.*
The writing's on the wall, lit morning and night.

x.

The characters that loiter or bivouac?

An Amazon, house arrest anklet, cargo
shorts, varsity jacket, skull cap pulled down.

The tiler, slater, mason, whatever he does
in a wife-beater and dog tags, so groomed
the kneepads down-gyved to his ankles blouse
his tear-away pants and sculpt a costume.
Ghetto gaucho, Cossack, Barbary corsair.

Also, the fellow selling incense, soap and oils.
In Burberry plaid Dhotis, tube socks, Timberlands.
Some days, beneath a kameez, it's camo salwars
tucked to combat boots. Other days, argyle socks,
gingham kurta, Ray Bans. Could be Samarkand,
not North Philly, the way he struts like stalwart
to a faith. God knows what time he's served,
for what, but he'll lord over the younger ex-con
converts. And who's to know if he really carried
out his Hajj or if a hennaed beard is just cool.

I've seen him drop his kid at the local charter
madrasah, same kid he schools all afternoon:
to ignore the customer who barters,
to palm the cash before he hands the soaps.
The boy is seven, with his crocheted kufi
and holds his wares like dayglo brass knucks.

The minor roles? A whole assortment of weird,
the things themselves, unaccommodated men,
one, poor, forked *Babalawo* reciting mysteries,
acerbic, with his beads, his bag, his shawl,
silhouette in fairy-tale, post-apocalyptic flick.

xi.

Another one I can see still
as I board on my way home,
and have seen him many times,
another prophet. An ailment
has him drooling, tongue
swollen, a tremor in his jaw,
the sort of existential puppet
or unnamed hero that just keeps
going on in Beckett's prose:
I who am on my way, words
bellying out of my sails,
am also that unthinkable ancestor...
He gets on after the underpass,
dressed up to the nines,
Panama hat, button-down
shirt, soaked, sure, but still
he'll mind his crease when
he leans back, crossing his leg,
and zeros in on whomever stares
and begins to rant, point,
or pontificate, as if holding court.
His, that same haut you know
from Cheney, Bush, Rumsfeld,
that same devil-may-care how
repugnant they come through.
Let Mad Meg tincture village
scenes with all the bizarrerie
which with no God or theology
boils to the *outré* in botched
procedure, the outlandish

in unpunished sin.
Like reflection of reflection,
the phantoms we pursue,
or those pixels that burned to
screens, he is faint in the dark,
as he stalks to accost a passerby
on a mission, with a job tonight,
in drag, turquoise velour gown,
foam crown. He's Lady Liberty,
handing out leaflets for the tax
outfit promising quick returns.
He sells loosies on the side and brindles
like the nonsense Goya etched
in aquatint to let pauper mirror
Ancien Régime, robed enigmas,
dark devils that mock and haunt.
The man exists, a graft of self
and symbol, like those hybrids
in myth which quarry the bad
in us, our gorging and excesses.
He stammers, hesitates, shuffles,
dressed in whatever is we stand for.

Corner

To chart this country, what better coordinates
than Wayne and Coulter, at the stoplight now,
when going northwest, a Chevy Impala coup—
detailed with racing stripe to match the neon
glowing from the undercarriage, rims spinning
to a distortion that gathers more momentum
every beat—is commandeered by a kid adjusting
his lycra du-rag in the rear-view mirror;
while going southeast, waiting for the light to change
and blasting another variant of beatboxing
and dub, albeit, without a dedicated subwoofer
amp, the kids from GFS, the private school
a few blocks east text away in a Mercedes.

What does Coetzee say? In a time out of time,
at either side of the divide you've got children
of paradise, fresh off swimming lesson, riding, ballet,
soft as *putti*, shinning with angelic light, fenced in.
Their innocence, the innocence of grubs,
bliss-filled, soul-stunned, abstracted, plump.
Like the lumpish, spoilt bullies in the last row,
they'll be promoted and rule the land.
Legitimacy they no longer trouble to claim, he says.
And then, their cousins on whom the first shade
of the prison house is already beginning to close,
rapacious, cruel, afraid of nothing, children of iron
of the times, snarled in the knags of violence.

There are other places, sure, ranches in Wyoming,
the shipping of Manhattan north and west,
bays and inlets, subdivisions near Scottsdale,
Point Reyes or the outer banks, the panoramic
of a sierra and Death valley, the souvenir shops,
hospitals, the epic mile on mile of sound barrier
shielding new developments all along I-95.
There is the map of the returns with its fat
middle, its well-oxygenated red states chocking
East and West, also the mock Calvaries
popping-up beside porn shops and strip bars
everywhere on interstates, Jesus camps,
and malls and multiplexes with five story screens.

Wayne and Coulter works: the red, gold
and green of the Rasta Bodega catty-cornered
to the halfway house, the Impala, *no white flags,*
no mercy I'm getting yo ass, the Mercedes pumping
another version, are neither emblems
nor metaphors, rhumbs for the north by northwest
slews the newspapers document each morning.
Be it AIG or holdup, budgets or graduation rates,
this agon of speaker power is as good a breviary
for where we are: a single pulse, with gas to burn,
blaring the same language, speaking in tongues,
with one kid going God knows where,
the others travelling the exact opposite direction.

II

Black Vesper's Pageants

—(after Cavafy)

> Il mio paradiso è la camera
> con vista sull'inferno alturi
> —Valerio Magrelli

If what wakes you of a sudden, past midnight
are the war or mating calls from roaming kids
as they rush across the street from trouble
or in trouble, you shouldn't dwell on plans
come unhinged, on how days you saved for
had another you in another city, on the done
for, the lost. Listen, the dash and sprint outside,
the ring of sticks or coins against the post
are undertow to the headlines that plot what
brokers wrecked, their pockets filled.
No illusion, what you've seen in the streets,
the sullen mouthed boys that pass you by,
the averted look, hooded gangs on corners
staring drivers down. The city is all too real
and you know it's broke when you can't tell
firecracker from gun, run-in from revelry.
Stand by the window, the kids disperse
like swarm from fire as a searchlight weaves in
and out, back and forth, a web around wrack
and ruin, an evanescent safeguard that judders
with the drum-roll of its thrust, like attendant
to a god entering a city it visits and destroys.

Alba

To prove the tenancies to beatitude transhumant
at the right time, the poor, the meek, the hungry show
through the glare like some front page photo pixelating
the faction of warzone, the destitution disasters out

for a week of coverage in the paper, the evening news.
But early morning, when we drag our trash cans out,
blacktop is tungsten, luster, lamina, blanches particular
existence and lets the contours of what was meant

efface what's here. Like fledging in myth, hatched in
a blaze, rising from its own cindery residue, the late Victorian
bad try at Utopia quickens in outline only, terraced
brick-fronts, sloping front yards, a monster of renewal

erected in a century when *those with nothing united
in common envy,* says Tocqueville; *those with some
in common fear.* Little has changed, the houses
one block down, falling, brick buckling, collapsed roofs,

pried keystones, missing pilasters, finials worked loose,
the sort of backdrop President enters for a photo-op,
hard hat and booties on, commiserating, promising help,
shaking hands, waving when motorcade hauls him away,

and leaving in his wake, the day to day, men with carts
or garbage bags, loading up rubbish, flues, drip edge,
siding. Let sun rise a bit, they'll be coasting from curb
to curb, bending down, reverent to recycling, trash.

Salvage

Because the place has to be empty
for a realtor to list, the owner's hired
muscle dragged all sorts of furniture
to the curb and drivers cruise and ask
how much for this or that, drive off.
Another antique dealer—a shop down
our street—is here to get first digs, show
what line splits rummage from ransack.
She's climbed into a room log-jammed
with odds and ends, tests her foothold,
totters on top of the uneven clutter, steps
astride two crates like some burlesque
colossus on a hunt for spares. Pay her
no mind, she'll crunch on stuff awhile.
There are souvenirs from war-torn countries,
a chimney garniture, Bustelli-wannabee
squires with hunting dogs and jackets and
three cornered hats, and other porcelain,
the odds and ends of services, tureens
and platters, cameo glass flowerpots
for a buffet or mantelpiece, mantelpieces
by the dozen, plain, fluted, ornate,
candelabra also, and the trampled
covers of *Rulah* and the *Green Lantern,*
a mildewed *Human Comedy* and wire
everywhere, like the mess of felled trees.
Bring it down, make me an offer is all
the owner says to anything we ask about,
just to shake his head, quadruple the price
and try to unload the property on us:

the terracotta Italianate façade,
the wooden floors. He thinks we're gay,
affluent, clueless, scoping a new enterprise.
He's a confidence man, a local selling
to tourists the patina of replicas as real.
We live within earshot of the avenue.
I tell him, and he knows *I* know and stops
or moves on to his life, the diabetes
that made his kidney fail, the dialyses
that wipe him out, the months he
convalesced and all the while, his *people*
cleaned him out, the good stuff,
a lifetime of work—Queen Anne doors
the painted slate mantels, vintage floral tile,
an entire canopy pub bar, the sacred
jimmied off lancet windows, God, angels.
He's middleman to desecration, in line
behind the guys boarding-up buildings,
on the receiving end of repossession,
just in front of squatters who move in,
a beneficiary from bankruptcy and foreclosure,
the one guys out on their luck will come to.
You see them at dawn, balancing piles
of leverings, radiators, downspouts, curbing
their shopping cart to wait his dispensation.
He wants to be a beach bum his remaining days,
talks theft and trespass, damage, trust,
as he sells something I've no name for.
Can you imagine him before his kidneys failed
in the leavings of dispersed congregations,
reading nostalgia's pulse? His counterpart
is upstairs still, greedy, unabashed. The orange
paws of her work gloves match the thong
that rides up when she hunkers down to grab.

Watch

As if vials, dime bags, spent condoms
didn't give away how Eros and Thanatos
earn street-cred on our curbs,

a Townwatch rap-sheet hits the inbox
with sightings of whores, details on hold-ups.
Someone reads police reports.

Renée logs on to a site that tallies crime
by zip-code. Karl, four houses down,
will film whatever fuss is loud enough to hear:

the sour of domestic outing, kids trashing
or defacing, after-school mischief he posts
on YouTube or Flickr, sends us links.

We must've done our share of prank
and injury, just steadied by mortgage
payments to prove our side of proprietary

prurient pumps the heart of civic.
It crossed my mind: *I'm the only one reading.*
No one cares about the black car, the blunts...

At least till the new couple posted:
an outcry, a *tout court* note
about *our* cats in their toddler's sandbox,

studded with a typographical arsenal
that twanged through a whole emotive
range, the sad of colon and open parenthesis

breaking down to the tearful semi-colon,
hyphen, semicolon, signing off with
the annoyed hyphen, period, hyphen.

That silence in the agora of Listserv
can't be cordial if the stuff that follows
when it breaks is anything to go by.

First reply, from funybunny@AOL,
subject: *your kid.* Body: an exclamation
mark flanked by double hyphens, the finger.

Then a flood of petty grievances gone
rank: *Music, weeds, dog shit, uncovered trash.*
The unkempt fronts, our property values,

unshoveled snow. Have pity on the strays.
Nothing too revealing surfaces about
the appetitive soul, but Pato's thymos,

the *amour-propre* thing, the passions
up for air will let you know why story
halts in Pentateuch with so many shalls,

so many shall nots. Neighbor has it in
for you, he's fidgeting with plus and minus,
wishing he had harakat and niqqud

on his keyboard to make his animus
grimace into cute. Like anyone with equity,
he'll need more than a prayer or a god.

Back Door

Somewhere between the hair product aisle
  and the Sista' Chips by the cashier
at WengWai's Convenience Mart where
  I saw them once stocking up on groceries,
there's a country we can maybe share,
  even if our apocalypses forecast bad
blowing in with different winds: theirs
  is Beast, horny, mother of abomination
on a fling with Plague, vials of wrath
  poured on a river and it becomes blood;
mine's a headline and the suspended
  particles dulling the creek in the park.

The outside of their house is wrecked
  and the inside isn't hard to guess
from the bubble wrap they stapled
  for insulation and curtains. Talk
has it that *home schooling* is just a euphemism
  for what they do to or with the kids,
that their seven beagles are locked-up
  on the third floor and the smell of shit
seeps through the bricks. Talk has it
  that she's suing the city on the grounds
the sink-hole they drove into blew
  a neural link to her husband's optic nerve.

For months, I saw him walk around with
  a cervical collar, then he put on
dark glasses to stop the double-light,
  shadow vision and did his rounds with
seeing-eye cane on hand. It's all I know
  for sure, beside the sickly oak we share

and are unable or unwilling to pay an arborist
    to chop. All I know beside the kid's projects
taped to their front door or propped near
    the fence: anxious communiqués,
hand-written, colored-in R.I.P's
    for the dead in the school shooting,

beribboned, cardboard dioramas to support
    our troops, collages of sincerity, slogans
cheering the unborn out of the womb
(UNBORN WOMEN HAVE RIGHTS TOO),
one liners to heroes, diptychs for the president
    triptychs saying no to referendum here.
The wreath they put out on Memorial Day
    gathered more catchphrases through the year.
What was it, his all apple, mine all fir?
    Though here the green in figure won't
explain away a fence, unless it weeds
    resentment and verdures over ill will,

unless it clears the small quibbles, the beefs,
    the gripes, slighted requests, short notes
slid under doors and windshield wipers:
    the barking and the smell, the front yard,
    the peeling stucco on the house, coming
    from everyone till the couple next to them just sue,
win, get the dogs removed, force them to sell.
    Before they go, they stake another monument,
a cross with the Beanie Baby version of a beagle
    nailed to it. Explain it to your three year old,
the crucifixion, the country we share beyond
    the industry that wakes us, our common ground.

Dietrologia

I learned an Italian term I hadn't known: *dietrologia*. The idea is that
many Italians believe that the surface or official explanation for something
can rarely be the real one. There's always something behind, or dietro,
that surface.

—*The Economist Online*

I meet him with his dog, a mutt he rescued
    and brought back to health.
I see him again, riding his bike, helmet on,
    in full regalia, Cinzano jersey,
lycra shorts, road-bike shoes. Again,
    I pass by him as he picks up trash.

First he'll talk about mange and ring-
    worm, then jobs;
then, he'll let bypass, diagnosis, dribble in,
    justify his work-out, his bike.
Then he inches-in with the mists that halo
    around the daily news, something

about the water, something about the soil
    eventually clears up to
a pile-up of conspiracies he walks me through.
    Who killed the electric car?
And who lets the aluminum and phosphate
    cabal pour fluoride in our glass?

I'm between peak-oil and international banks
        in the obligations of chitchat,
the short end of courtesy, the daily news
        and the *Fortean Times*.
The trails of condensation aren't just
        high octane burning that clots

on contact, but possibly sylphs—not nymphs
        in the woods—Parcelasian
spirits shed of their commetary body to dwell
        in the air and heard the poisons,
turn them by some spagyric miracle into rain
        which statistics show...

These are the downsides to syntax and plot,
        poor guides to the perplexed,
with so many cladistic offshoots yielding
        a hopeful monster in every branch.
It's business or pleasure up there, I say,
        and why conspire when low

dishonest decade seems like euphemism
        for what folk will get away
with in the open, spotlight of a press conference?
        He wants my e-mail.
The obligations of chitchat, the short end
        of courtesy. He sends

a satellite picture from some moderate
        resolution image
spectrodiometer to prove, as far as I can
        tell, a day of take-offs
and landings leaves the continental US
        looking like a chalkboard

after school, the light wash of white
        everywhere, X's and Y's
multiple persistent strokes bleeding
        through with the lessons
of torn itineraries, the erratic of the Hénon
        map, a litany of departures.

I don't reply. Next, a link to the Post-it
        revolution: *basically, he says,*
you get yourself a pad of Post-it notes,
        you know, the little yellow
sticky notes, a black marker and then
        start leaving the public

little subliminal messages, for example:
        When you go to buy fruit
and you're at major supermarket chains,
        leave a note near fruit and veg
which reads, DONT BUY GMO,
        or go to the egg section and

leave a note, FREE THE CHICKENS, lol.
        It's like figting the establishment
with a billion paper cuts. I don't reply.
        He's trying, I know,
an eloquence for things not being what they are,
        saying the back of the in-flight

magazine with its world strung by parabolic
        ganglia stemming from hubs
means subterfuge and harm. Netchaev
        and Weil, Tea Party patriot
hum the same tune on a different off key,
        hoping you reply, confess,

convert, put masking tape on the laptop's
      web-cam, monitor the media,
he writes again, as if to dodge the shadow
      of fuselage could deny, by all means,
that the glossy in-flight cover is so well thumbed,
      you could lift our prints.

Three Houses Down

—*after Juan Gelman*

Forgive the statistical candor,

there's no great poem in undoing.

Of the thirteen children he begat,

eleven are locked up, the one girl

turned tricks for crack on Wayne

and, in turn, gave birth to seven.

Three live there; the rest scattered

with uncles, cousins, their fathers

maybe. She's on the wagon now,

the mom, born-again, going steady.

Forgive the geographic accuracy,

in my daughter's interactive globe,

when you press the stylus to a Congo

or a Sudan, regardless of how broke

the people there are, how fractured,

a happy synthesized tune will chime.

For us you'll get, any given time,

Oh! Susanna or Yankee-Doodle-Dandy,

and so might be misled by the sanctioned

olden-days version of ourselves.

The music is other that rattles transom

from the gas pumps on the corner.

So I take it block by block I guess,

if it helps explain three houses down.

He bought the semi-detached to get

the kids out off Hansberry, understood,

a street where bang for the buck

has live ammunition in the chambers,

in the sort of straits where a move

one block up north is as upward

a mobility as anyone can afford.

Bear with the anthropological turn,

the elementary forms of kinship,

all those symmetries and reciprocities

that whole generalized exchange

is so much more toe-tagged, snarled

and fraught, what relations came

to stay a month, few weeks and vanish,

the kids could not tell for whom exactly

police barged in, if to arrest or question.

Forgive the histories. They won't explain,

however much you backtrack on their

wrongs, though we like to, for comfort's

sake, to explain away mom on the corner,

Papi, trying to do good for the kids,

unleashing his invective on them, the *fucks*

and *you shits* that echo through the block.

Memorial

for the earth is filled with violence
                                        —Gen VI. 13.

A damp season, they'll seem like fungal spread
on posts, a blight best understood in statistic
and crime report, crawling to cover the thick
of staples left to rust from lesser posting, yard
sale, lost cat, runaway dog. Lately, mind you,
a bit more desperate, more out of work, less
high-tech, signs folks scribble offering to do
odd jobs, junk pick-ups, garden work, my favorite
rides to prison. Who needs a headline or speech
when state of the union is rigged-jobbed
to the creosote soaked poles on every corner?
Americans Must Mourn, Make-do, this one
says while the *Times* and *Couriers* elsewhere
sugarcoat what's fit to print. Churrigueresque
gone pop, they are, the piles of plush animals
meant to grieve the seventeen year-old shot down
on the corner, Queen Lane and Green, Alvin
the Chipmunk, strapped by the neck, Sponge
Bob wire-tied above, Daffy and also the generic
fauna spawn in sweatshop elsewhere meant
for fair or dollar bins, plush teddies, lucky dogs,
eglantine owls, Noah's every beast, every creeping
thing of the earth after his kind, it seems, left
to tuft and mildew after rain, blanch in the sun.

Block-Party

Here:
The Republican ex-marine who blasts
Lynrd Skynrd in Germantown;
the couple who chill to Modest Mouse;
the opera buff; and the bachelor who owns
one album only, or so it sounds.

I've known them by music that drifts out
their windows come spring, choruses
that moan as they turn ignition keys,
the slow core country-tinged vocalise,
the growls and blast beats on a minor key.

By their flags—a rainbow, the Earth,
the Semper Fi—their bumper stickers
sometimes or campaign signs they stake
in sidewalk planters or wire-tie to porch.
Who *are* they? At the *First Annual* [sic]

Pot-Luck Block-Party, if nothing else,
we'll figure what we do. Some hand out
their card, Dr. William Neshiwat,
Director of Legislation, Bruce Botwin,
Real Estate Broker, Pedro turns out to be

a Civil Service Commissioner. Even Bill,
who fled the towers coming down,
shell-shocked he says, unemployed since,
will give his out. As always I come up
empty in this potlatch of title or career.

I see him midmornings when I walk the dogs.
Hunched, gloves and gardening hat on,
he combs the sidewalk brick by brick,
picks handfuls of green and brushes
what's left back into shape, explains:

Some stuff makes it look quaint, some stuff
I'll not abide; it's bad for my reputation.
His length is a herringbone latticework
of micro-saxifrage, that puts all to shame.
Today he shows off his pets, *his babies,*

leashed to either shoulder, a Sisserou
on one, an African Grey Parrot on the other.
Later he'll bring his turtle for the kids to pet.
For the time being, he parades like a pirate
dreamt up by Ralph Lauren or GQ.

We peeled the aluminum and plastic wrap
from tray, platter, bowl, and spread out
a smorgasbord of food issues. The vegans
brought their tofu dogs. The vegetarians
tossed some cranberry quinoa mess.

The supermarket omnivores bought
two tin-foil roasting pans of fried chicken
at Pathmark. There is more, brownies,
pie, cookies, bean salads and greens.
Some orbit by the table and pick.

Mothers heap starch and protein
on their kids' plates, hover over play
with forkfuls or juice. We cordoned off
the street with caution tape,
lined trash cans like talismans

via Rubbermaid to keep the kids safe,
drink our wine in peace. Weather,
the news, toddlers and TV, mosquitoes
or dry basements are foreplay to things
that make us come as one: women

servicing their Johns in our backyards,
the dude who walks his pit-bull
off leash, noise from the station.
There are micro-factoids, overshares.
Thom's father might die anytime.

Pat tried a diet pill that had her hiding
in the closet. Ross stumbled into a site...
No *E detto l'ho perché doler ti debbia.*
Enough to stray to other circles.
Who are they? What are we? Who's we?

Here: The Sufi couple and their brood;
the Rutgers prof and husband in training
for a triathlon, they say;
the self-appointed block captain
we didn't know we had. Here also:

his rival who began assailing mailboxes
with printouts to launch a campaign:
Explorer of life, nature lover, photographer,
wife, swears she'll turn the block more connected,
sustainable. Nicole will ambush her,

offer clipboard, make her sign a petition
to evict the guys in the impromptu half-way
house beside hers. Here: Chair, co-chair,
secretary and treasurer of the neighborhood
association, ready with their speeches

the challenges ahead, the current momentum.
Here also, the woman with the yappy
little white dog, though she moved out
after some deal. We heard she signed
deed over to her son in-law, not here.

Julie also, who won't pick after her dog,
won't stop, drags it and leaves
a trail of shit. She is block stalwart
today, asking we show at the hearing
voice our feelings on the vacant next to her.

Depends who you ask, back in the day
she called the cops on the guy next door,
reported what serfdom he submitted
his impaired sister to. Cops took her away.
Depends who you ask, he funneled

funds for the IRA, published this or that,
might've even smuggled gelignite for them.
One thing is sure, if she called or not,
something pissed him just enough to move,
stick it to her, let the property go rot.

We're little more than hearsay, what partition
yields beyond the up and down the stairs,
vacuum cleaners, power tools. Tidings
bleed the party wall, a rebus pieced
from roar, confession, phone call.

That I'll kill the cats, might mean it.
That I'll leave. That answering machine
fends off collection agency. Lots more,
enough, some mornings neighbor realigns
the self that ghosts me from a bit of late night

with the self he trusted with his keys.
We have heard of conversions,
roads to Patmos or to Mecca,
and the hostilities that propelled them,
of Mrs. Lee who found out secretary was

Mr. Lee's chosen route to perdition
took the high road and began to spread
Adventist intel door-to-door.
Those are the salt licks of gossip.
There are larger detonations: kids on PCP,

wives airing the sour of marriage on sidewalk.
Suzanne (occupation unknown) and Jim,
the artist fellow are the most recent specimens,
despite appearances, despite the nuclear family,
lets-found-a-country, mortar-a-community,

pass tax-cuts on this picture-perfect harmony
they put on today. They hold hands,
keep Roy and Katie in tow, seem germ
to commercial republic and apparel catalogs
that go with it. Fit, young, with a job.

But the day they came back home to find it
burglarized, with the police taking reports
after she reckoned what was left, what was taken,
Suzanne shifted registers as she turned
from itemized list—her mom's jewels,

laptop, the kids stuffed toy, Christ's sake—
and let name of the Lord be slippery-slope
to the hell of scores she kept on her husband:
his salary, his art, his mother, the place
he moved them to, Christ's sake.

No-shows make a snug catalog for *ubi sunts*.
The Sayers, Matt, Stacy, where have they gone?
Where is Fred and Deborah? The Kellers?
The Matusovs, who hardly say hello but scope
what yard work or DIY project anyone has going,

have L&I on their speed dial, where, oh where
is that concerned neighbor conservationist quick?
And Ramona, who bought the restored house
with Mr. James but went MIA shortly after—
what made her go? Karl and Robin?

Old-timers, the Gillfillans and the Bironts
sent their fucked-up kids instead.
David, forty, snapping too many candids
of the children; Phil, honorable discharge,
drop out, introduced himself three times.

There are some eat-and-runs.
The contractor walked his wife over, grabbed
a drumstick and left. A month ago, he cut
semi-circles from two sheathing boards,
hinged them, slapped primer on

and wrote, all caps and bold, his own
commandments of good neighborly behavior,
propped them in his front yard.
Thou shall not screech that note again,
refrain from projects after10:00 p.m.

Thou shall not blast your porn ...
You would notice, we exchange recipes,
buy ice-cream from the truck, talk breweries
or tax-hikes not half a block away
from the last public housing high-rise

and yet the sliver in the pie chart
that is our demographic includes
none of *them*, though few cut through,
folks who scavenge for aluminum in our bins,
wake us up at night, foray to the *A plus,*

line up for the Power Ball.
They check us out, do a double take on
who we are, the kids around John's sulcata tortoise,
we with the sad playlist of middle age
our impro DJ chose to soundtrack our talk with—

The Beatles, Aretha, Norah Jones.
Too many poems about parties blast music,
pile empties, oblige a quick last minute run
to stock up and gather momentum
on the full swing of fist fight or dance floor.

Poem will detail what psychedelic synthed riff
syncopates into a mantric, tantric tempo
and let the promiscuous *pasodobles*
cast shadows in the likes of Shiva and Shakti.
Some even end on bonfire fueled sky high

as the congregation feeds it an outdoor couch.
We are in the cryptic of occupations (Civil
Service Commissioner? Director of Legislation?)
our kids asking us to get them a pet turtle now,
at that common place Aristotle thanked his lucky

stars for being born into, *that best political
community, the propertied class, its unlettered laws,*
the heart of civic. This poem will end in tears.
Not yet. First a speech, a cordial agitprop
from the co-chair about the Facebook page,

the two dead copper beeches (a danger all around),
the need to work the ground, get together,
a potential Halloween parade, how urgent
it is we volunteer, yea; not till she is done
recruiting for the scut work that keeps polities alive,

stuffing envelops, knocking doors to spread
the contentions that make us a union,
the connect the dots of who we are,
dot of mortgage to dot of bad job,
dot of car payment to tuitions

and what debt we shored to have a stake—
though we might as well find our counterpart
in those *hidalgos* come to less, scrambling
to save face, clinging to station,
will fight you for the parking spot.

Speech done, we dither between recycling
and trash with paper plates, plastic forks,
and peel the butcher paper
from the fold out tables and scatter,
go inside to bedtime stories, TV time.

We'll meet again around accident
or incident, ask more details from the cops.
Some straggle, stash the wine box,
have that late-party thrust, that look that taints
heavy-drinker, hanger on. I'm there and

so is EJ and Joanne and Bill and Bill's partner
Jeff who refused plastic and has lorded over
with Reidel goblet in hand. He jokes about
his kids, *Sort of functional,* he says about Sally
his thirty-something, *for Manhattan at least.*

Joanne is all ears, ready for what confidence
too many wines will yield. His failed marriage,
the commute to and from Manhattan where
Bill can't set foot and so to be with him
he'll put on the mileage but regardless,

Bill cuddles the turtle to his chest all night.
The pet is indiscretion now, living
adumbration of what *the* public arena means
and fresh off chemo and radiation, a full recovery
so far, Joanne is in that tender, hypersensitive

mode that lets her *understand*. She is mother
right now, she is also Calvin, Rousseau, Marx
in embryo, principled, taking sides, pulls
away and whispers. In that sort of playground
clique, in huddle and pinky-swear, in the dark

of asides, legitimacy and legality are born.
It's the monster come of us together
when we talk of animals we harbor in our lives.
The turtle by the way, just to bring it full-circle,
the turtle brings the three of them to tears.

Blizzard

Inside, yet another American poem propped
the angel of history to its armature, not Klee's
wide-eyed scare-crowish Samothrace exactly,

Benjamin's *wreckage upon wreckage, Paradisal
wind-storms.* As if guy-wired to the stanza,
the long-shot exegesis and all its hot air

would fend the buzzards of insignificance
hovering in the quotidian that poem transcribes.
Outside, what weatherman forecast days ago

grew to big wet flakes, toughened to a powdery
zero-visibility waft, like fog closing behind freighter.
Relentless, the front, we can hear us in it:

the thick slosh of tire-treads on pavement
like tack peeling; the sound-proofing that dampens
city's usual din, a final modulation as snow squeals

under the weight of cars, turns crust, craqueleure.
Nothing like history, this storm, nor progress
either, more rift before calving, at least in that

pitch of tire chewing through; more a mad censor
raging at what's disordered and deboshed, the sort
that'll airbrush blemishes, turns trash a blank

and doing so, turns us, coming from work,
shadows of who we are, huddled, hooded, blurred,
as if coming or going from another world, drifting

through the gradations between home and refuge.
Let storm be storm, dump its two feet on us.
The angels of history, fallen though they be,

will rise tomorrow and plow out cars.
write large with a cindery pitch on blank, leave
chairs, cones, trashcans to claim their spot.

III

Summary

—after Valerio Magrelli

All said and done, for every foot
of majesty in the humpback breaching,
there's forty of proglittid adding
to the stobila of the tapeworm,

miles on end of herring-, screw-,
round-worms, cyclospora, giardia,
trichinia, liver flukes, and kissing bugs.
Hookworm larva wisp in the blood.

There's also the cone plant's stemless
perennial lumps noshing on leaf litter,
clionaid sponges boring into shell
and rendering a filigreed brittle lace

that's the minute version of pock-
marks a Colt AR-15 will bore into walls
of captured towns, Mogadishu, Kabul.
In sarcoma's seeming sexual itch

you can hear something like music
arguing, in its very logic, its own end,
hear suspended subdominants, nonchord
tones disperse in serial, aleatoric, micro-

tonal effervescences fizzing everywhere
in the body of sound, the close-grained
spruce of Cremonas, the alveolar whirl
of woodwind. A tonal catastrophe,

history, arrhythmic cells, superfetation,
ambush, hold up, what lymphoma does.
And look at the land and sea, captives
to a guest that's armed and dangerous.

Theory & Praxis

> A shudder in the loins engenders there
> The broken wall
> > —Yeats

For late capitalism, there is that truck again,
its plush animal bungeed to the grill, Taz
or Mickey, take your pick, grinning as vehicle
barrels out of the hidden loading ramp
of new corporate headquarters. It'd kill you
despite its blue beacon and its beep.
For late capitalism and its art, go in the lobby
where the winter garden's pride and joy
is a two thousand square foot high-def
LED screen that chameleons to paneling,
morphs to wood grain, pauses, begins again.
Betty Boop doing the Lindy Hop back and forth
to a looped sample of tin-pan-alley spliced over
breakbeat. She's black and white but casts
a bright red shadow, distorted silhouette, half
amoeba, half spinning top. The oldest living
flapper on the respirator of nostalgia, under
marketing's knife could be a Blakean emanation
the way she keeps crowds of tourists rapt..

That's the posh of Center City. In the park,
my neighborhood park, other's *get a room*
means kids might as well stock up on Pampers,
buy a stroller, get a crib. But to sociologist—
eminent, top tier—it's the cool of teenage
pregnancy, out of wedlock births, without

a nod to the pimply lusts of adolescent self.
Who doesn't harbor some memory
of making out in cemeteries or empty lots?
Three explanations he purports instead.
One: that *street* families share a *cultural
code* whereby sex is a way of preening.
Two: that by having children early, the poor
are *preempting the high infant mortality rates
associated with bad healthcare.* He's serious.

No wonder these guys sit through lecture,
sip cold white wine and chat away
the prison house of language, the ends
of history, like hoodwinked prelates in the remote
province of tenure track with outsized egos
and little faith, laser pointer to smart board
mumbling *episteme, pastiche, hyper-reality,
simulacra.* The ten million pixels in seamless
flat array the corporate honchos walk under day
after day, they ironize. Trompe l'oeil of nebulae
are twirling now, Betty Boop having poofed
away on the last beat. I figure, dust
the obsolescence out of oliprance to render
just how gaudy, how vulgarly stocks and bonds
ruffle with profits, how brandishing the electric
bill alone would make bling look prudent.
Figure one of them sneaks *panem et circenses*
or *prolefeed.* They nod to the real in quotes.

As for the paper's architecture desk,
they quivered with superlatives instead, *glorious,
sublime, The Comcast Experience, most stunning,
the images, so realistic you think they jump
off the wall, an artistic achievement.*

A wave recedes and the moist sand turns
wood again. Folks gasp when Bugs Bunny
shakes himself into a world of been seen.
There's more. Overhead, in the eight stories
of empty real estate that make a glass atrium,
some gawk at Jonathan Borofsky's
Humanity in Motion, which consists of ten
life-size pop homages, play-dough hues
of human figures walking across
horizontal girders, soaring at different levels.
From nowhere to the dead-end of plate glass
on a twelve inch beam and a ten floor drop,
· briefcases in hand and no one bothered to say,
really, facsimiles of secretary and junior exec,
will it not hint of corporate tight rope, have
someone think, no safety net or dead ends,
have the slightest hint of bird on windowpane?

Late capitalism for you, the garbage truck
pulling off, the panes, the kids in the park,
a guy theorizing—that's what he's paid to do—
what the boy's getting to in the park,
he'd call climax. Kid, having learned his chops
from *Gangland* and *Be My Bitch* would call it cum.
Three, *the poverty of relationships thesis* says
young girls get pregnant to make up for
what went amiss with father, mother, teacher,
fill the void so to speak, give and get affection.
He never rode the 23, seen sixteen year old,
ear buds on, texting, haul toddler, choice words
for the kid *shut the fuck up,* never seen backslap.
He is then, what's disturbing about language,

what's awry with *our* conversation,
the wrongdoing in knowing swabs around
the wound, blind to irreversible, to cause
and effect with all its quotation marks, its
simulacra this, simulacra that. Here's simulacra,
the old shoot-them-up chase of old updated
by these six year olds, one's on the ground
the other's pointing with a branch, saying,
how I wish this were an AK-47, I'd blow your brains out.
The alarms are off. The gate is shutting behind
the garbage truck, leaving just the whiff of rancid
in Center City. In the park, the other kid is done,
zipping up, walking away, girl rights herself.

Testimony

The tongue-tied, broken English of the Chinese
woman talking to the judge takes garble beyond

the mumbled, the butchered and back to its root
as in to sift or cleanse, as in to rid grain from chaff,

as in *all sorts of spices be garbled after the deal is made.*
That's Richard Haycklut on Alexandria, in the OED,

as he roughs out the *ways never known before,* sketches
where spices grow, the things we have appetite unto, and grafts

onto English one more term schooled in the peddle
and hawk of entrepôt or souk or docks.

Richard Ligon follows, falls *a coughing* in Barbados
as long as the *garbling* of red pepper's going on.

In the backwash of his wake, Yariko plucks Inkle
out of the deep just to sell her down the river,

literally auction her off to grind in the knocking room
of ingenio and then to an afterlife of myth. Yes this *back*

*and forth from tropikes to both poles without a doubt
of profit* is birthing archetypes and fable, noble savages

and Calibans, operatic betrayals, broad side ballads,
a whole new language which the plaintiff here

is struggling through, having refused a court appointed
translator out of distrust or hubris, who knows.

I'm here as witness, though I know next to nothing
and it's hard to tell whether her stalling, her second

thoughts are mere unease on what a word might mean
or just her riddling how she has gotten here

to aftermath, filing for custody because her husband
took their three year old, over two months ago and

there are no certain whereabouts, won't be brought back.
So she's touring us through dropped calls from Kansas

or Arkansas (she doesn't know) credit card bills
with charges from filling stations in Omaha

or Oklahoma (she can't remember), the country,
an index of off-rhyme and assonance

where a house her husband supposedly bought her
fits somewhere, a split-level, vinyl-sided generic,

where all these detours, these scenic uncertainties
dead end like all American dreams, a subdivision,

a cul-de-sac conceived on purblind faith alone.
She has charted the whole thing and is our cicerone.

Maestro Dante niggles; *Maestro* he'll hound Vergil
for answers and that's just as he loses his footing

in the scrap heap of irreversibles that's afterlife.
Imagine then the descent into someone's marriage,

a left to *la città dolente,* a right to *l'etterno dolore*
with wailing kids in tow to learn slap from slug,

slight from smart, and the rationale behind dissembling
and sabotage. Did I mention she's due next week,

that all she can muster to the Judge's whys
is a sort of confused quote? Why did she let him

take the girl? *So kid see America. To buy house.*
Her husband told her, *to visit family and friends.*

This is the unconjugated of ordeal, of the ongoing
and we cannot tell, in their apartment, *short* from *shot*

from *shout.* Though the friends have surfaced.
We nailed Oklahoma, and because she's backtracked

to a far off courtship, pieced together his two
tours of duty in Vietnam, return visits across Asia,

prolonged stays, the same in and out nomadic zeal
of missionary or merchant. *Stript and rifled of all,*

left destitute, Ligon writes, *found myself a stranger*
in my own country, I embarked to any other part

of the world. You've seen guys out on their luck,
the sort that safety-pin a MIA/POW flag

to the back of denim vests, stake a corner
and set up sandwich boards with clippings on

conspiracies and all, limping back and forth,
as if *Philoctetes* role had not been cast.

Not hard to understand, why some
would vanish, dissolve like unfired clay in basins

flooded by nothing but past circumstance,
going over landscape. Your bamboo is his snare;

a cover bridge, ambush he needs to loiter round.
Necessity, the Greeks called it, the Venn diagram

lassoing stuff world throws at us and our bewildered
response. The thing is, in the reckonings of escape,

there's so much meticulous adding up, food and drink,
the native's pastime, the kind of fruit tree, the hound

and river, that I can't help but think of subterfuge
and *prayers for parts unknown* doing little but masquerade

how mercenary makes a killing, closes in on the *skinnes,
the Golde, the spices, the precious stones,* all while he lusts

after *the colour yellowish, the hair black for the most part,*
dicks the native. Can't tell pilgrimage from crusade,

abscondence from return and though she is talking
now the subtropical humid of Guilin, their marriage

there, with the précis of his wanderings on hand,
with so many blanks between honorable discharge

and his re-emergence decades later, I'm thinking
how English bulked up with new fevers, fabrics,

rhymes, how the mail order bride factors in
the animus soldier stockpiles during action,

divided selves in doubled worlds that we all are.
He miss America. She imagined a backyard

a house, the faux-*Gemutlich* of suburbia I guess
but ended up in some courtyard apartment,

a section-eight affair law mandates be gated
and still the shrubs sprout hypodermics nightly,

dime bag and red caps strew patches of grass.
She made do, found a park, took the kid there

while he collected whatever check and sent her
to tutor Mandarin at some pricey private school

where no one bothered to check for a green card
he wouldn't get her, wanting government

to keep no record of him. Another evasion
more dodging and sidestepping, though double-parked

beemers picking kids up, the triple parked Volvos
dropping them off are complicit, harboring

so to speak illegal aliens, throwing twenty dollars
on top of twenty grand yearly tuition because they know

the circumnavigations buck has made and figure
in not as explicit a way, but figure, let the kid

quarry the soft core Quaker sweat-shop here,
get to know its lexicons, its ranks, its negligence

so later she can make a killing from the hard core
furnaces that extrude plastics and profit.

The Primum Mobile of the whole, Ligon in full
hyperbolic dispatch on *ingenios* circa 1673,

*in all of these there are great casualties, with goudges
sockets, sweeps, cogs, bray-trees, and when all that*

is done, the casualties at sea to be considered.
I'm here as witness, know next to nothing,

here to tell that I've seen her with her daughter
at the playground, seen she's a good mother.

Otherwise, the fist-size crater on the dry-wall,
the month-long silent treatments, the lock-ins

and lockouts, the under-the-table pay he garnishes
to fund the trip that disappears the kid,

might as well be furniture dragged
in some upstairs where there is not telling

what or why, except here the lug has the drag
of larger cargo, yeah Matteo Ricci to Matteo Ripa,

the hull crazed, Hamburger Hill, vandal, reformer
agent provocateurs and defenders of the faith,

confidence men, their doings and undoings
ravening, predatory, caring little what mix of seed

or beast or wretch is struck off the bill of landing,
plucking enough benisons from third heavens

to put Eve to shame and deforesting on top of that,
on top of that, fallen Adams that they are

unable to name. They pecked the lexicons of creoles
to rig and shimmy a new Babel, a rhyme rich macaronian.

Think muscovado/Mikado, viva, Shiva, Kava, Java.
Think those birds weaving torn grocery bags

silicone caulk and bits of milk carton to their nest.
Vehicular and transitive Emerson says of speech

as good as ferries and horses for conveyance
but do not try abiding there might be his ultimate advice.

And yet Cuihua is home right now, in the halting, hesitant,
broken English, trying to detail all the bits and pieces

of what's been done, the why's and whereabouts,
trying to rehearse her husband's last night home.

American Beauty

Iconic, Hoffman as the skinny, fuck-up
breast-strokes in the welter of chlorinated silence,
unperturbed, in a sort solipsism only womb
affords, even if the water is meant
to ripple like the raw, tense nerve of the *zeitgeist*,
the whole sexual revolution thing, the Cold War,
the angst in affluence, some existential itch.

He'll be midwifed back by a catchphrase,
Plastics, there's a great future in plastics,
though, fuck-up, nonconformist, his days
won't end in the perfunctory of molecular weights,
of casting and extrusion. But still civilizations
will rise from Playmobil; whole economies
bubble around Barbie. Enter, thirty years down,

another film dwelling again on the anomie
of surfeit, sounding the shallows of the suburbs,
feeling the pulse of those who've wrecked there.
In this one, the troublemaker, the malcontent
gainsays the whole thing and offers as respite
the grainy, hand-held video of a plastic bag
pirouetting to wind, down an alley, by a brick wall,

like the one stray leaf left from some Sibylline
frantic scattering, its oracular pronouncement
writ large, *Plastics, there a great future's in plastics.*
I've seen them carried by the wind, like fledglings
from a nest that's the lot outside Family Dollar,
whole flocks jut, spin, swerve, rip, figure eight—
a wake of flaccid vultures over carcass.

Sibylline, the dumb prescience etched
in Aeolian sandblast, ventifact, yardang,
what the future is really, you can double on it.
Wind refilling loess, beds of gravel and loam
everywhere, Europe, China, the Midwest,
even if there's plenty left, *remarkable alluvium
filled with shells,* I read, the abrasive emery

it makes on getting there, as absolute as amnesia.
You can hear it toil in cold fronts, the sort
with gusts topping 50 miles per hour,
the relentless karabiners frapping flagpoles,
the Tyvek on a block worth of construction site.
It's like the panic of a clapper that has you praying

morning come and come morning,
what will be left of us also, I think,
our sheddings outside Rite Aids and the Gap,
the bags, ballooned up and snagged, more than ten
per tree I swear, puffed up windsocks wind-bagging
the logos, the bull's eyes, the shields,
the smiley face, the pumas, the swoosh.

Also Available from **saturnalia books**:

A spell of songs by Peter Jay Shippy

No Object by Natalie Shapero

Nowhere Fast by William Kulik

Arco Iris by Sarah Vap

The Girls of Peculiar by Catherine Pierce

Xing by Debora Kuan

Other Romes by Derek Mong

Faulkner's Rosary by Sarah Vap

Gurlesque: the new grrly, grotesque, burlesque poetics edited by Lara Glenum and
Arielle Greenberg

Tsim Tsum by Sabrina Orah Mark

Hush Sessions by Kristi Maxwell

Days of Unwilling by Cal Bedient

Letters to Poets: Conversations about Poetics, Politics, and Community
edited by Jennifer Firestone and Dana Teen Lomax

Artist/Poet Collaboration Series:

Velleity's Shade by Star Black / Artwork by Bill Knott
Polytheogamy by Timothy Liu / Artwork by Greg Drasler
Midnights by Jane Miller / Artwork by Beverly Pepper
Stigmata Errata Etcetera by Bill Knott / Artwork by Star Black
Ing Grish by John Yau / Artwork by Thomas Nozkowski
Blackboards by Tomaz Salamun / Artwork by Metka Krasovec

Winners of the Saturnalia Books Poetry Prize:

Thieves in the Afterlife by Kendra DeColo
Lullaby (with Exit Sign) by Hadara Bar-Nadav
My Scarlet Ways by Tanya Larkin
The Little Office of the Immaculate Conception by Martha Silano
Personification by Margaret Ronda
To the Bone by Sebastian Agudelo
Famous Last Words by Catherine Pierce
Dummy Fire by Sarah Vap
Correspondence by Kathleen Graber
The Babies by Sabrina Orah Mark

Each Chartered Street was printed using the font Adobe Garamond Pro and Arial Narrow.

www.saturnaliabooks.org